PRO FOOTBALL
★ MEGASTARS 1995 ★

Bruce Weber

SCHOLASTIC INC.

New York   Toronto   London   Auckland   Sydney

CONTENTS

Photo Credits
Cover: (Newton) Sportschrome East/West; (Bledsoe) Allsport USA/Scott Halleran; (Barry Sanders) Focus on Sports; (Deion Sanders) Allsport USA/Scott Halleran. **4:** Sportschrome/Rich Kane. **6, 12, 24:** Sportschrome/Vincent Maniello. **8:** Todd Rosenberg. **10:** Allsport USA/Stephen Dunn. **14:** Allsport USA/Rick Stewart. **16, 22, 30:** Focus on Sports. **18:** Focus on Sports/Tony Toneic. **20:** Sportschrome/Rob Tringali. **26:** Allsport USA/Mike Powell. **28:** Sportschrome/Eric Metcalf.

ISBN 0-590-53527-7
Copyright © 1995 by Scholastic Inc.
All rights reserved. Published by Scholastic Inc.

12 11 10 9 8 7 6 5 4 3 2 1   5 6 7 8 9/9 0/0
                                                              34
Printed in the U.S.A.
First Scholastic printing, September 1995
Book design: Doug Klein

"Hey, Coach. What kind of season did you have?"

"Well, we were nine and seven."

"Hmmm, nine and seven. A winning year. Not bad."

"Yeah, right. Hey, everybody was nine and seven."

And that, dear friends, is the story of the National Football League. Seven of the 28 teams, one-quarter of the entire league, finished 9–7. The whole NFC Central finished 9–7 (except for Tampa Bay, which never has a winning season), and all four 9–7 teams made the playoffs. Advantage: Fans in Green Bay, Minnesota, Chicago, Detroit, New York, Kansas City, and Los Angeles stayed interested through the final weekend. Disadvantage: Except for fans of teams like San Francisco, Dallas, and Pittsburgh, it was a ho-hum season of ups and downs.

The prime example: the New York Giants. Coach Dan Reeves' men won their first three, lost their next seven, then won their final six for their 9–7. They missed the playoffs when Tampa Bay, as expected, lost their season finale to Green Bay.

Now comes 1995 with new faces, new cities, and new chances for mediocre teams to qualify for post-season play. Say hello to Jacksonville and Charlotte. In north Florida, the Jaguars are playing in the totally revamped Gator Bowl and figure to capitalize on the intense football interest spurred by the college game at nearby Florida and Florida State.

The Carolina Panthers, headquartered in Charlotte, North Carolina, will actually spend their first couple of seasons at Clemson University in South Carolina, while their new stadium is built.

Incidentally, for students who normally struggle in geography, you have plenty of company in the NFL office. The Jacksonville Jaguars, with the Atlantic Ocean rumbling just a few miles from the Gator Bowl, open their football lives in the AFC Central. And the Carolina Panthers are slotted in (where else?) the NFC *West*!

Although the expansion rules are more liberal than they've been and free-agency makes more prime talent available than ever before, chances are the newcomers will hover near the bottom of their respective divisions until they can hope for 9–7—and mediocrity.

This year's edition of *Pro Football Megastars* might require a little explanation for new readers. Before you write angry letters to the publisher, please be assured that several of our choices were made with the past—and the future—in mind. No doubt that Steve Young remains the NFL's premier quarterback. Junior Seau continues to menace Charger opponents from his roving linebacker spot. When he's healthy, Michael Irvin is still one of the most dangerous wide receivers in the league.

But we decided to introduce some of the lesser-known, up-and-coming talents to you. That's why Drew Bledsoe is our 1995 quarterback. Many NFL experts figure that the New England Patriots will be the next AFC power, thanks in large measure to the coaching and player selection of Coach Bill Parcells. If the Pats reach that level, Bledsoe will lead them there. Same with the New York Jets outside linebacker Mo Lewis, a young standout who's hampered by playing for the AFC East doormats.

Looking ahead to the season, we anticipate little change at the top. Dallas and San Francisco will continue to dominate the NFC—and, hence, the NFL. Teams with aging quarterbacks, like Miami, Kansas City, and Minnesota, may not enjoy the success they experienced in '94. The Giants, whose quarterback Dave Brown survived his first year as a starter in fine style, should improve.

The neck injury to wide receiver Sterling Sharpe in last year's season-ender could have major implications for Green Bay. Pittsburgh, with a defense that isn't quite as good as the Steel Curtain of the late 1970s (ask your dad about it), still is good enough to lead the AFC again. How good could the Steelers and San Diego Chargers be with better quarterbacking?

Will last year's have-nots—Houston, Cincinnati, and Washington—make major comebacks in '95? Which new coaches will prove to be the superstars like Pittsburgh's Bill Cowher and Chicago's Dave Wannstedt?

That's why they play the games—and with two new franchises opening for business, there will be more than ever before. Scoring figures to increase, putting more pressure on defenses everywhere. It should be fun. Enjoy!

—Bruce Weber

DREW BLEDSOE
QUARTERBACK
NEW ENGLAND PATRIOTS

★ DREW—OR FALSE? ★

Some folks in the Foxboro (Massachusetts) neighborhood might not believe it. But there are experts who make their living in the NFL who believe that the Patriots are the AFC's next powerhouse. Now, that doesn't mean much in the overall scheme of things. Just ask the Denver Broncos and Buffalo Bills, who won a whole bunch of AFC titles without ever winning the big one. Still, with Bill Parcells—the owner of a pair of Super Bowl rings—at the coaching helm, anything's possible.

If the Pats rise to that level, Drew Bledsoe will drive them there. Although there's some excellent talent on the New England roster, Bledsoe is "The Franchise." If you didn't know about Drew until he became the Patriots'—and the NFL's—number-one draft pick in 1993, it was probably an accident of geography. The 6'5", 235-pound quarterback played his college football at Washington State, and the Cougars aren't exactly a staple of college football telecasts. So when Drew announced his intention to file for the draft following his junior year, fans across the nation immediately began doing their homework.

Parcells had the first pick overall and pondered his options. The Pats could pick up all sorts of live bodies in exchange for the premier selection. And they needed them. But Parcells, who developed young Phil Simms into a Super Bowl winner, saw no other option. You start building with your quarterback.

As always, Parcells was right on the money. Drew started his pro career on the road against one of his boyhood heroes, the Bills' Jim Kelly. And though he threw for a pair of scores, he was a so-so 14 for 30 and only 148 yards. But fans saw enough to get them excited. Drew didn't let them down.

He still hasn't. Lots of folks figured the Pats would be better in '94. But few expected them to challenge for a playoff berth and the AFC East title. Surprise! When Drew tossed a three-yard TD pass to Leroy Thompson in the final 2½ minutes of the Pats' 13–3 season-ending victory over the Chicago Bears, all of New England cheered. It capped a spectacular second season for Bledsoe.

New England had suffered through an awful 5–11 season (including a 1–11 start) in Bledsoe's rookie year, then began '94 at 3–6. But, without much of a running game and a so-so defense, Parcells allowed Drew to throw as often as he liked, as the Pats rallied to win their final seven games to finish at 10–6.

Bledsoe's 691 pass attempts blew away the all-time mark (655) set in 1991 by Warren Moon. His 400 completions were just four shy of Moon's record. He hit Ben Coates three times in the finale, giving Coates the all-time single-season record for receptions by a tight end (96).

If Bledsoe had anything to prove, he did it on the next-to-last week of the season. Playing at Buffalo, against the four-time Super Bowl Bills, Drew hit on 22 of 31 passes for 276 yards (and no interceptions). New England came from being behind 17–3 by scoring 38 unanswered points as the Pats ended the Bills' run, 41–17.

Bledsoe's strong-arm tactics surprised a lot of folks. When he was winning a pair of Super Bowls with the New York Giants, Coach Parcells favored strong defense, a smash-mouth running game, and ball-control passing. But times—and personnel—change, so when Bledsoe threw the ball 51 times (32 completions for 421 yards) in the '94 opener against Miami, it signaled a new game plan. A few weeks later he hit on 45 of 70 passes, both NFL records, against Minnesota. The last completion was an overtime 14-yard TD to Kevin Turner that capped a 26–20 victory for the Pats. They had trailed 20–0 before Drew cranked it up.

Drew is exactly what New England has been waiting for. The Patriots have won in the past, even went to a Super Bowl. But unlike the region's other teams (Celtics, Red Sox, and Bruins), the Pats have never had a superstar. Bledsoe could be the man. And he works at it. While most pros do what they can do to avoid their fans, Bledsoe actually seeks them out. He's a people person.

That's why he still spends part of every off-season back home in Washington, dressing in jeans and sneakers, and hanging with his old high school buddies.

On the field, Bledsoe likes to set goals. "in '93, I was satisfied with getting better every week," he says. "Coming into the '94 season, I wanted to be able to play at a level that would allow our team to win." And that he did—big time!

EMMITT SMITH
RUNNING BACK
DALLAS COWBOYS

When you pass through Pensacola, Florida, be sure to stop in Emmitt Smith's sports memorabilia store. There you'll meet most of his family. That's important to Emmitt. While most pro football players hire pros to run their businesses, Emmitt J. Smith III turned to his mom, dad, three brothers, and two sisters. He wants to be just another guy. Of course, that's really impossible. Carrying a football, which most folks simply can't do, Emmitt J. Smith III is number one.

Nobody knows that more than the Dallas Cowboys. When Emmitt is in their lineup, they win about 80% of their games. When he's out, they don't win. Smith has missed three games during his Dallas career (two in a contract dispute, one—the 1994 finale—with an injury). The 'Boys' record in those three is 0–3.

There's something special about Emmitt. You know, warm and cuddly and friendly. His image is so positive yet, unlike other superstars, he doesn't seem to work at it. It's just him.

Of course, it pays to have talent and Emmitt has plenty. Only Barry Sanders' incredible season prevented Emmitt from winning his fourth consecutive NFL rushing title in '94. Even so, despite missing the Cowboys' last game, he wound up with 1,410 yards and ran for 20 touchdowns. He added another on a pass reception. His 21 six-pointers in 15 games easily captured the league title.

Still, Emmitt was upset about losing the rushing title. When he sat out the finale, reporters grilled him on the subject. "Hey, I'm a running back," said Smith. "And I can't run. If I can't run, I'm just a back. And I'm not just a back." Emmitt's testiness surprised more than a few folks. Smith dreams of being remembered as one of the all-time greats. And he knew that Jim Brown of the Cleveland Browns had won five consecutive rushing titles between 1957 and 1961. That was the record Emmitt was shooting for.

It doesn't matter. Despite being a mid-first-round draft pick (number 17) out of the University of Florida in 1990, Emmitt was an instant hit in Dallas. Cowboy assistant Joe Brodsky, who throws around compliments like manhole covers, speaks lovingly about his best tailback. "Unless Emmitt's career is shortened by injury, he'll be remembered as one of the all-timers." Period.

Smith's secret for success may lie in his thighs. They're like tree stumps. The 5'9", 210-pound Emmitt is built low to the ground and when those thighs churn, he's almost impossible to bring down. Opponents get solid hits on Emmitt about as often as the San Diego Padres win baseball games. When he went down in '94, it was a non-contact, pulled hamstring that sidelined him.

Smith wasn't pleased about missing the last game. He has that greatest of all pro football reputations: "Plays hurt." The previous year against the Giants, also in the season finale, he excelled despite a shoulder separation that would have benched most NFL running backs. The victory gave the 'Boys the division title, a first-round playoff bye, and home field advantage throughout the playoffs. That may have been the most significant step on the way to their victory in Super Bowl XXVIII.

If Emmitt has any regrets, it's the fact that he left Florida after his junior year and still hasn't earned his degree. "I'm about 15 credits short," he says, "and I'm going to get that degree." But he uses that fact to motivate others. "Education is important not only to me," he tells young people, "but to my family. I'm going to get my degree because I owe that honor to my mother and father."

Emmitt is accustomed to being in the spotlight. In high school, he took a program (Escambia High) that had never won and made it a winner. At Florida, he gained 1,000 yards in his first seven games as a freshman—and finished in the top 10 in Heisman Trophy balloting that season. As a pro, he's 5-for-5 in Pro Bowl selections, won the NFL MVP Award, earned two straight Super Bowl rings, and made more money than he could have ever dreamed about as a kid.

But what Emmitt J. Smith III wants to be is number one—of all time! He has a serious shot.

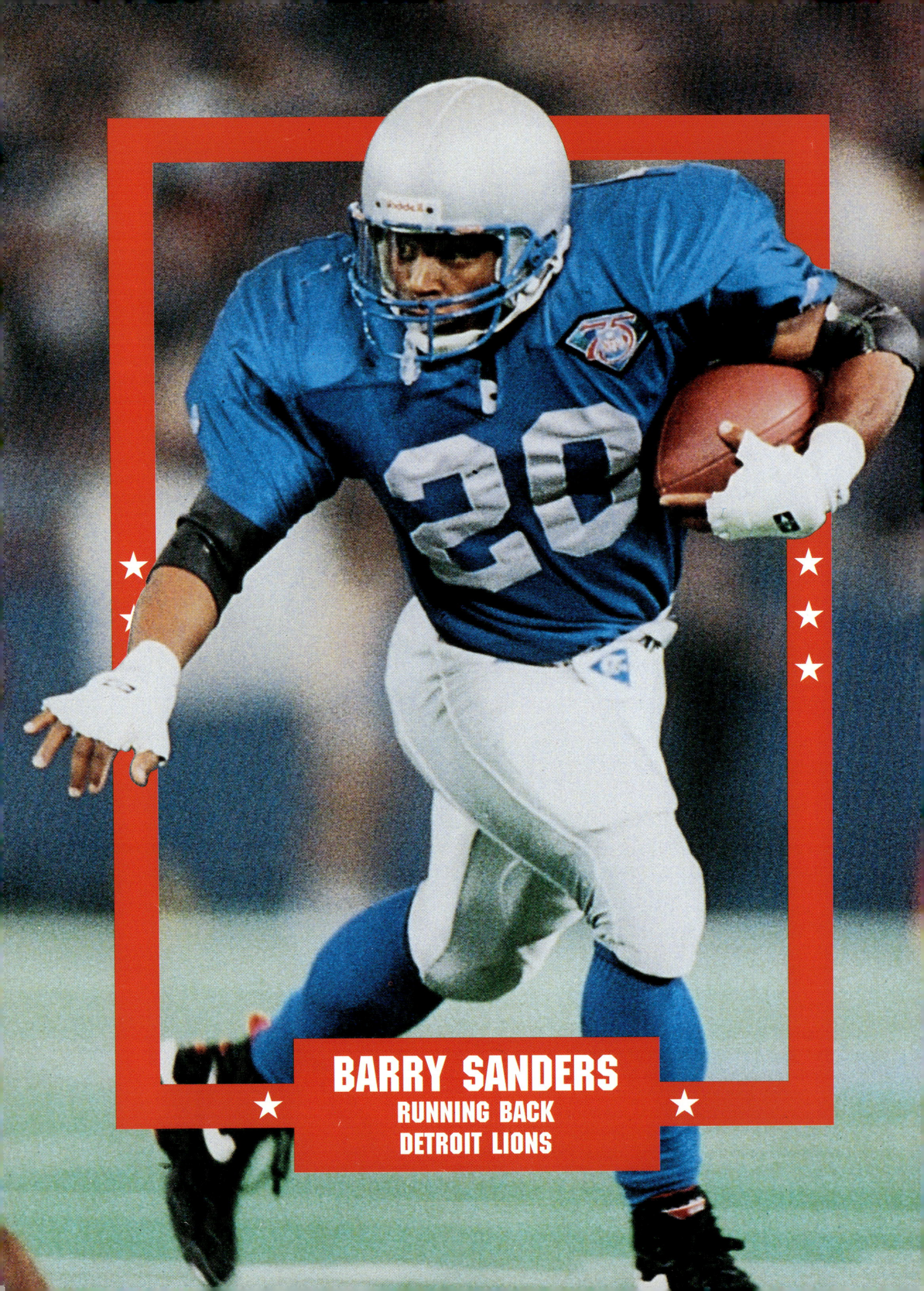

BARRY SANDERS
RUNNING BACK
DETROIT LIONS

I f you watch a Detroit Lions game tape, you get the idea that it was produced by the Hollywood guys who made *The Invisible Man.* Opposing defenders draw a bead on running back Barry Sanders and reach out to wrap him up. But like the ghostly invisible man, he simply isn't there. A move here, a slide there, and he's gone. Most football fans prefer to watch their favorite team so they can root it home. People who love football watch the Lions so they can be entertained by Sanders.

The 1994 regular season ended with Barry standing on the sidelines of a 27–20 Detroit loss to Miami. Barry looked disappointed, though he told the press that he wasn't. The Dolphins defense, rarely frightening to NFL opponents, had limited Sanders to 52 yards on 12 carries. The fact was that Miami had scored early and often, forcing Detroit to throw instead of run. That left Barry with 1,883 yards on 331 carries, 117 yards short of the coveted 2,000-yard mark. Only Eric Dickerson (2,105 in 1984) and O.J. Simpson (2,003 in 1973) had ever done that.

Still, '94 (except for that minus-one-yard game in the wild-card playoffs) was the year Barry Sanders really came of age. He'd been a Pro Bowler before; now he was measured against the all-time megastars.

The 1988 Heisman Trophy winner at Oklahoma State, Barry was the Lions' top draft pick in '89. He made an instant impact on the Motor City, becoming one of only two NFL rushers to gain 1,000 or more yards in each of his first six seasons. Despite the weekly pounding, he managed to stay healthy, missing only two games, until a partially torn left knee ligament sidelined him late in the '93 season.

But he was back at full strength last year, ready to lead the Lions and, if the rumor mill was right, to save Coach Wayne Fontes' job. If he had to prove anything to anybody, he did it during the third weekend of the season. On a national Monday night telecast, Barry squared off against the Dallas Cowboys. Early in the first half, he zipped into the line and hit a brick wall. There was no hole. Most backs would have gone down in a heap. Not Barry Sanders.

He hopped backwards and darted to the left, only to be trapped by Cowboy defenders. So he coiled his body and shot straight ahead—and gained three yards. Only three yards. But for veteran football watchers, it was one of the most impressive gymnastic feats they'd ever seen.

If Barry had any shortcomings in his game last season, it was the fact that he didn't score many touchdowns. With seven, he finished tied for 20th in the NFL six-point race. But Sanders also tossed off runs of 85, 84, 69, 63, and 62 yards. That's a career for most normal megastars.

Barry Sanders, of course, isn't your normal megastar. For him, 100-yard games are almost routine. But how he gets his yardage is even more impressive than the numbers themselves. If you love art, buy a Lions' highlight tape from NFL Films and run it in slow motion. You probably won't believe your eyes. Sanders looks more like a rhythmic dancer than a football player.

"Barry is truly a work of art," says his All-Pro teammate, wide receiver Herman Moore. "And he does it so naturally. If I tried to do the things he does, I'd probably wind up on injured reserve."

Sanders' teammates all have special memories of his successes. They argue about which move was his greatest. "It was the Saints game, that 40-yard TD after being hit by three guys," says one. "No, it was the run in the Dallas game in '91, when he left Ken Norton, Jr., grasping for air," counters another. "Are you kidding?" says a third. "It was that play against Buffalo when he landed on his helmet, got up without his knee touching the ground, and took off in the other direction!"

There's no correct answer. All you know is that you have to watch Barry carefully. The next play may bring the move that will start the next highlight reel.

Sanders is out there with the all-time geniuses of the game. You simply can't believe what he has just done. But perhaps ABC-TV's Dan Dierdorf put it best when he watched that hop-and-shoot run against Dallas last September. Dierdorf's comment: "Wow!" That's about it.

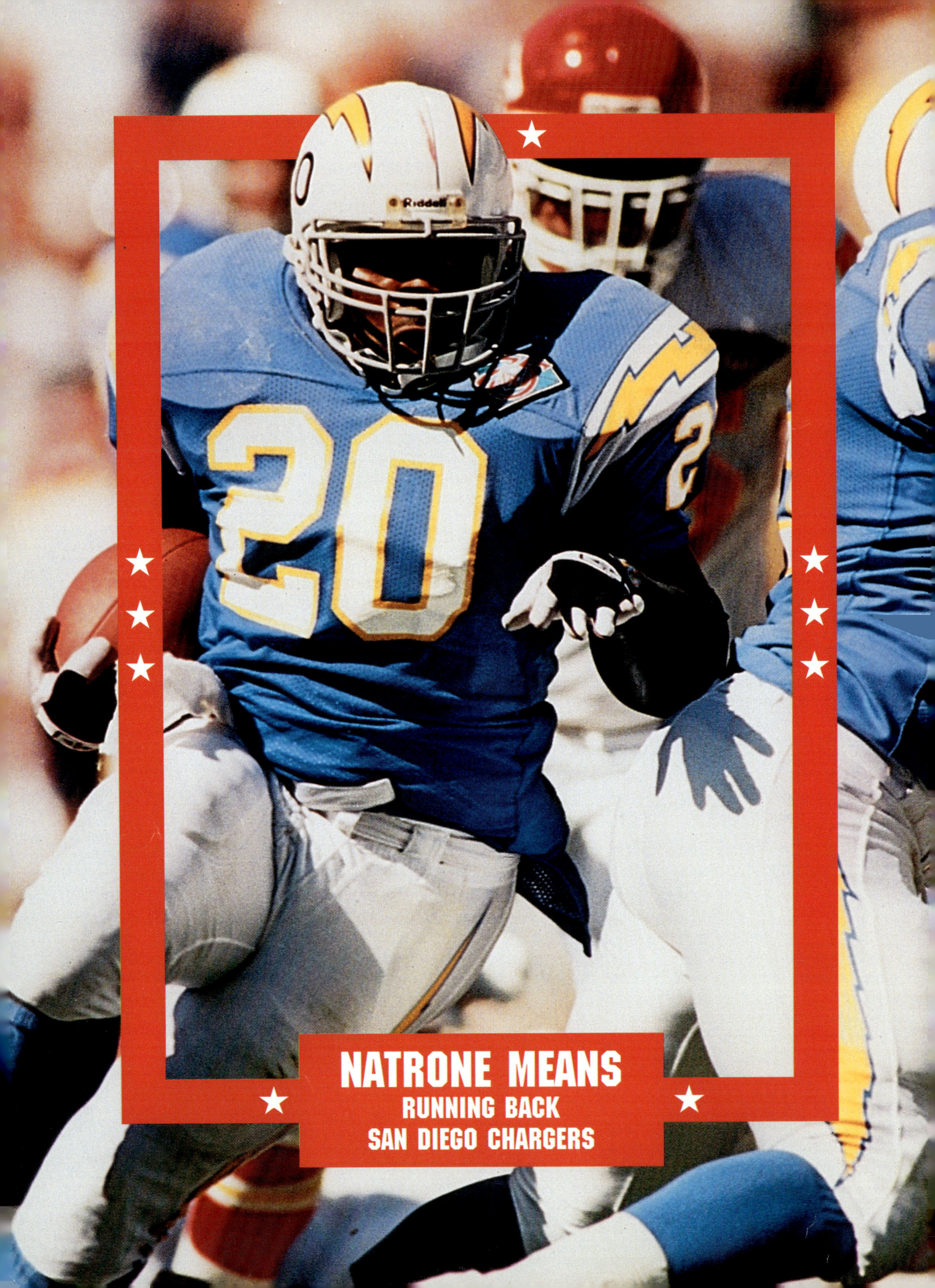

NATRONE MEANS
RUNNING BACK
SAN DIEGO CHARGERS

★ NATRONE MEANS BUSINESS ★

On a Monday or a Tuesday or any day up to Saturday, you might mistake Natrone Means for one of the San Diego Chargers' ballboys or gofers. He takes the phrase "California casual" very seriously. He dresses that way, he ambles that way, he jokes that way. But, as the old song goes, "never, never on a Sunday."

On the nation's day of rest, Natrone never rests. He checks casual at the door, puts on his game face, and gets as serious as anyone in the NFL. In San Diego on a fall Sunday, Natrone Means business.

And what that means is that Charger general manager Bob Beathard and coach Bobby Ross are two really intelligent dudes. They dealt one of San Diego's all-time runners, two-time Pro Bowler Marion Butts, to the New England Patriots in April 1994. Some Charger-watchers thought they were nuts. But credit the duo with great vision. During Means' rookie year, they saw glimpses of how good Natrone could be. Publicly, they said they traded Butts to get under the salary cap. Privately, they believed they were taking the club up a notch. "We felt," said Beathard, "that he could do some things that Butts couldn't."

There were signs. As a rookie, Means was getting increased playing time. He was the club's number-two rusher with 645 yards. He led the team with six touchdowns. He had a couple of 100+ yard rushing games. He was getting more of the key fourth-quarter playing time. And so the move was made. Means' performance—and the Chargers' AFC West championship—proved it was right on.

The credit for Means' success in '94 needs to be shared. In addition to the wisdom of Ross and Beathard, there was the mentoring of running backs coach Sylvester Croom, improved front-line blocking, and better personnel all around. But it was Natrone himself who really made it happen.

"He was so much more focused this time," says Coach Croom. "He never doubted he could do it, but he had a lot to prove. He was excited as a rookie, but this was different. He prepared better for each game, watched what he ate, and got a lot of rest. He was ready."

He had to be. Charger quarterbacks handed him the ball 343 times, about 22 carries per game. Those are the numbers of a Barry Sanders or an Emmitt Smith. And while his total yardage wasn't in the Smith or Sanders area, his 1,350 yards were second in the AFC to Seattle's Chris Warren. The only player in the NFL with more rushing touchdowns was Dallas' Smith.

In the season finale against Pittsburgh, Natrone had a typical day with 22 carries, 85 yards, and 2 scores. That produced a 37–34 victory over Central champ Pittsburgh and the West crown. Just another business day for Means.

What the Chargers love most about Means is his versatility. At 5'10" and 240 pounds, he fits the bill as a perfect big back, the punishing runner who gets the hard yards up the middle. But Natrone can also take the ball outside, drop a shoulder, shake a hip, and leave potential tacklers grasping at air. His teammates marvel at his confidence.

Wide receiver Shawn Jefferson is a big fan. "Natrone comes into the huddle and says, 'You guys block, take care of your man, and I'll do the rest.'" And he usually does.

Means' critics point at his attitude, which sometimes sounds like self-praise. He was once quoted as saying, "I'm going to be better than Emmitt Smith." And then he laughed. Trouble was, the reporters forgot to report the laugh.

"They've got him wrong," says Coach Ross. "It's not arrogance or bragging or even cockiness. It's just confidence and he's earned it. Remember, he could have been a college redshirt senior in '94. Instead he was the AFC's number-two rusher."

"I can't explain it," says Means, when questioned about his success. "I guess I'm just blessed. I just go out there and run the ball. I do what I have to do. Hey, I've got to pay the bills at the end of the month."

He shouldn't have trouble doing that for a long time!

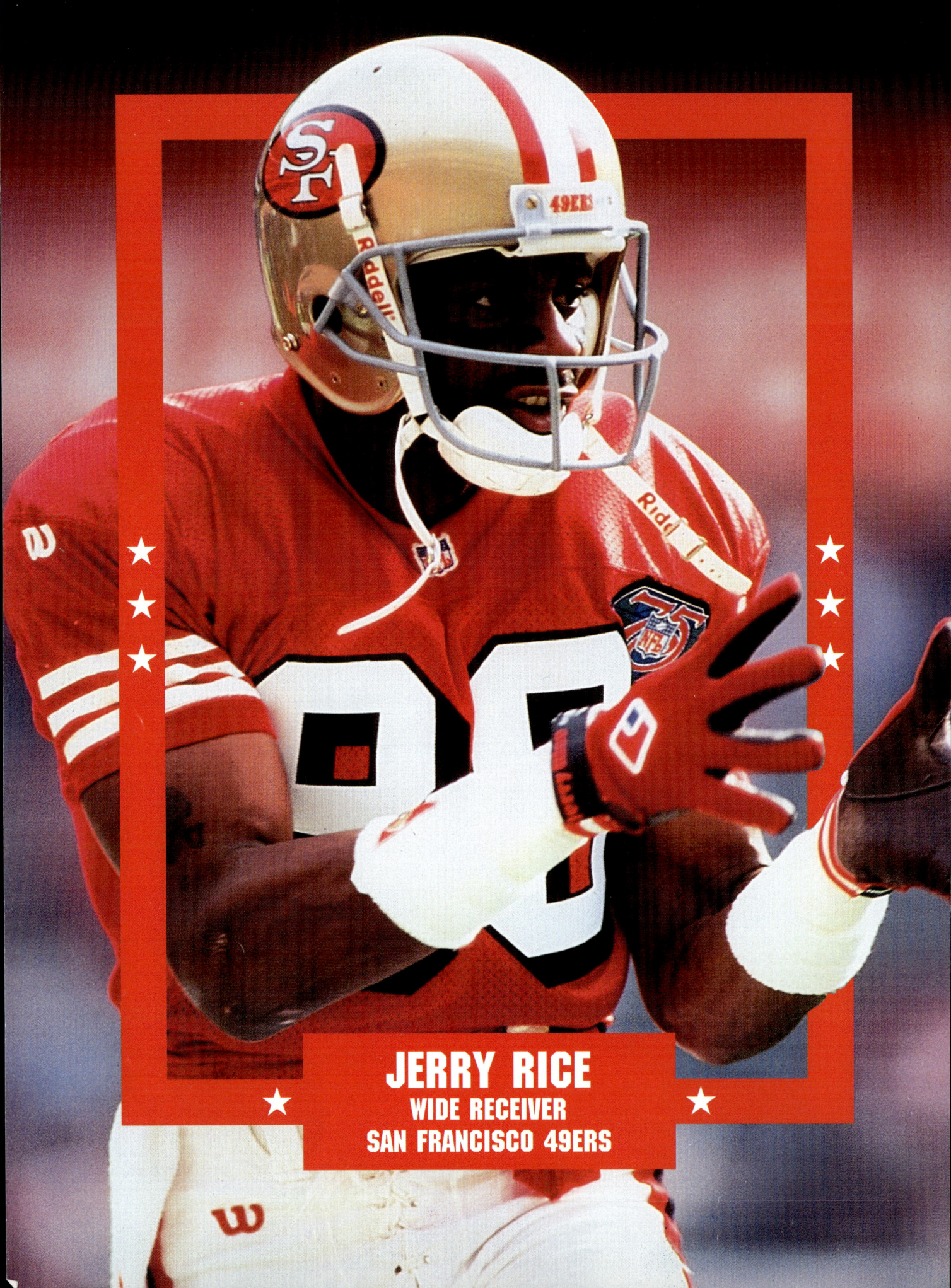

JERRY RICE
WIDE RECEIVER
SAN FRANCISCO 49ERS

★ SIMPLY THE GREATEST ★

At almost any position, you can argue about the identity of the number-one player. At quarterback, it's Steve Young, or maybe Troy Aikman with Drew Bledsoe coming fast. At tight end, it's Ben Coates—or perhaps Brent Jones or Jay Novacek. The best cornerback is Deion Sanders—or possibly Rod Woodson. At running back, Barry Sanders is tops—or is it Emmitt Smith?

At wide receiver, however, there's never an argument. The San Francisco 49ers' Jerry Rice is easily the best in the game. He may well be the best player at any position. He may even be the greatest player ever. That's the only question.

It is unofficial pro football policy that when a superstar changes the way a position is played, everyone tries to imitate. Since Nate Newton made the offensive guard position his own, other teams are looking for talented round men to play guard. Lawrence Taylor, with speed and a body like a cat's, altered the way outside linebackers rushed the passer. Everyone now looks for OLBs that look like LT.

There isn't a coach who wouldn't love to have a receiver who plays like Rice. Trouble is, no one plays like Rice. He isn't the fastest wideout in the league, but he does own deceptive speed. He isn't the flashiest receiver in the business, but he can do more with a short pass than anyone who's ever played the game. He isn't the biggest guy on the outside, but he's blessed with a body that an Olympic sprinter would die to have.

Everybody knows the Rice saga. He grew up in poverty in a small town in Mississippi, then played his college football at Mississippi Valley State in Itta Bena, far off the pro scouts' beaten track. But the scouts heard plenty about him and when he starred in several post-season all-star games, he attracted plenty of attention. The 'Niners traded up in the draft to get him. That was one of the wisest choices of all time.

By the time he's done, he'll own most of the records in the NFL book. He already has a bunch of them. When the New York Jets' Art Monk set a new mark for consecutive games with a pass reception late last season, he admitted that "it isn't my record. I'm just holding it for Jerry Rice."

Jerry's 12 TD catches in '94 (he also ran for a pair of scores) padded his all-time lead. In 10 seasons, he has caught 130 six-pointers, 30 more

than previous record-holder Steve Largent. And Largent used 14 seasons to earn his mark. With three touchdowns in last year's season opener against the L.A. Raiders, Rice passed Hall of Famer Jim Brown in the overall TD race. Jerry has now scored 138 times, 12 more than Brown's old mark.

The rest of his career numbers put him in position to justify our impression that he's the greatest player ever. Though Minnesota's Cris Carter set an all-time record with 119 receptions in '94, he'll have to keep doing it for a decade or so to catch Jerry. Rice grabbed 108 passes for 1,466 yards last season, giving him career totals of 816 catches for 13,242 yards. He should pass all-time leader James Lofton (14,004) sometime around mid-season. How impressive is Rice's performance? Lofton took 16 seasons to do what Jerry will do in 10½!

What's the secret of Rice's success? Obviously, sheer physical talent is a key. You don't do what he does without overwhelming ability. He runs like an Olympic sprinter and owns one of the softest pair of hands ever seen on a football field.

But Jerry and everyone who watches the 'Niners credit his work ethic for his ongoing high-quality performance. Rice will turn 33 in October. That's the age when many of the great ones began losing it. No one expects Jerry to turn off the jets.

"I think I'm in better shape now than when I came into the league," says Rice, who works harder during the off-season than most players work during the year. There's a steep hill near the 'Niners' old training camp at Redwood City, California. He knows it takes lungs, legs, and guts to assault it and he only does it about 10 times a season. But he tackles it. And his regimen includes numerous sprints and a strict year-round diet.

At a time when many begin winding down, Jerry insists, "I think I'm now at the top of my game."

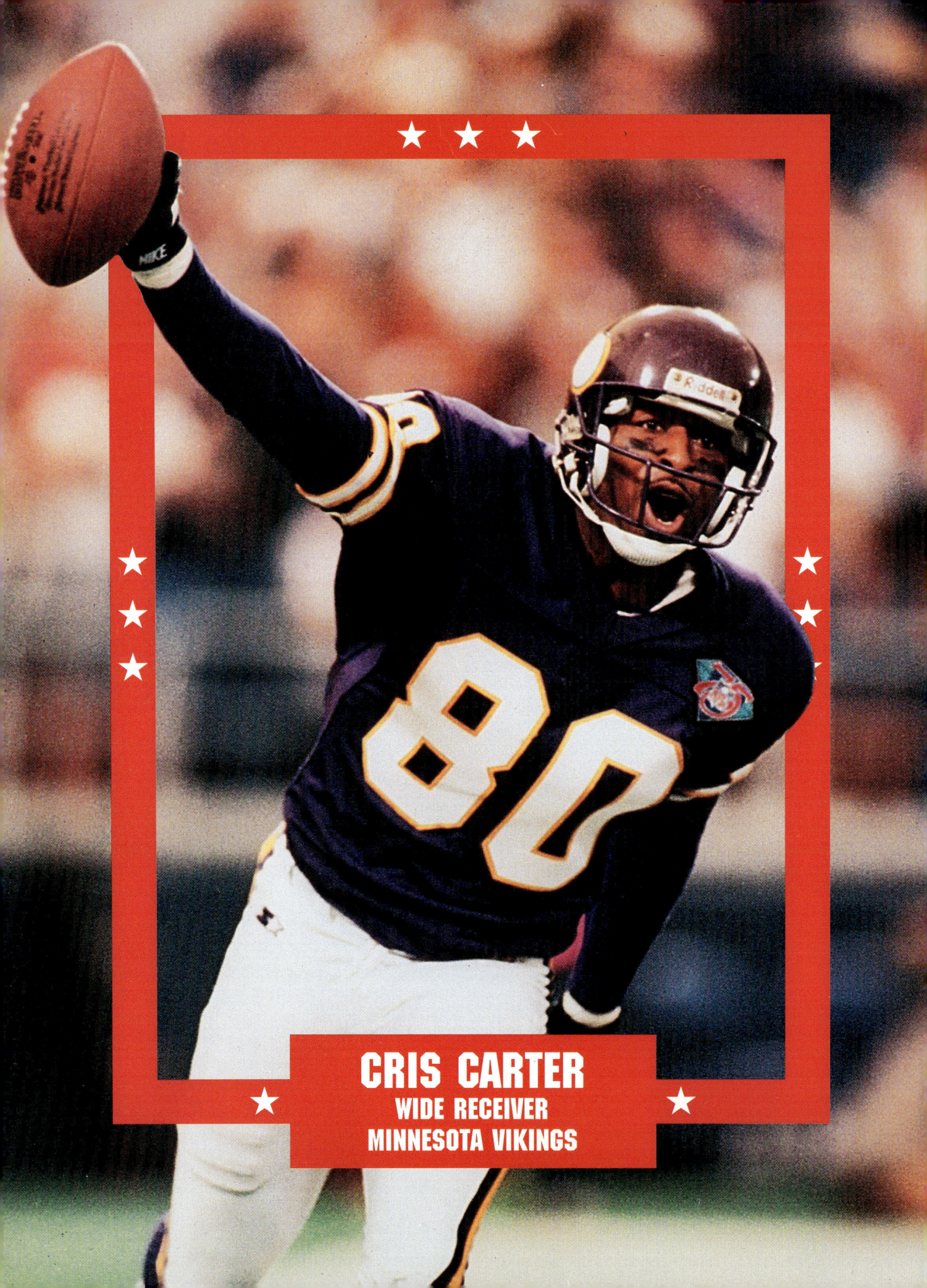

CRIS CARTER
WIDE RECEIVER
MINNESOTA VIKINGS

★ BUDDY'S BIG MISTAKE ★

t was almost too easy, like grabbing candy on Halloween. Minnesota Viking QB Warren Moon would drop back to pass and Cris Carter would make the catch. Fourteen times the pair hooked up, adding 167 yards to Moon's passing totals and Carter's receiving summary. And to Cris Carter, they were the 14 most satisfying catches of his career.

It was just a little matter of revenge. On the opposite sideline stood Buddy Ryan, head coach of the Arizona Cardinals. Five seasons earlier, Ryan, then coach of the Philadelphia Eagles, had called Carter into his office. "You can stay here in Philadelphia, if you want to," Ryan told the one-time Ohio State superstar. "But you're going to be my number-three wide receiver."

"Thanks, but no thanks," answered Carter, who was instantly cut by the Eagles. Both the New York Giants and the Vikings bid for his services. Carter chose Minnesota and it changed his life. During the 1994 season, he caught 122 passes (for 1,256 yards), easily destroying Sterling Sharpe's old record of 112 catches.

Ryan did more than cut Carter. He woke him up. "I had been something of a party animal in Philadelphia," says Cris. "I rarely thought about what I ate, what I drank, or what I did to my body. That all changed the day I arrived in Minnesota."

Cris' wife, Melanie, agrees. "He has always been a good and sweet person," she says. "But his life is more focused now. He is a much more peaceful person."

That's not the only fortunate thing that happened to Carter. While the other productive receivers have been blessed with outstanding quarterbacks, Cris has worked with some of the most mediocre in the game. Jerry Rice had Joe Montana and Steve Young, former record-holder Sharpe had Brett Favre, Michael Irvin had Troy Aikman. Carter had to be content with such non-standouts as Sean Salisbury, Jim McMahon, Rich Gannon, and Wade Wilson.

So when the Minnesota Vikings went shopping for a premier quarterback before the '94 season, Carter was hoping they'd come up with the right one. They did. Although the Vikes hotly pursued former Miami backup Scott Mitchell, they dropped out of the bidding at around $11 million. They left that problem to the Detroit Lions. Then they went after Warren Moon of the Houston Oilers and he wound up turning the Viking—and Carter—fortunes around.

Cris' amazing '94 season was the result of a combination of factors. First, of course, was Moon. Then the NFL announced that the no-chuck rule—DBs can't hit a receiver more than five yards past the line of scrimmage—would be strictly enforced. Third, the Vikings came up with a crew of receivers that could take some of the pressure and coverage off Carter. By season's end, Carter had his 122 catches and partner, Jake Reed, had 85. Their total of 207 easily eclipsed the old two-man record of 190 set by Haywood Jeffires and Drew Hill of the Houston Oilers—and quarterback Warren Moon!

Carter's success secret is his amazing athletic ability. "He makes those exciting acrobatic catches," says Viking coach Dennis Green. "If he can get a finger or a hand on the ball, it's a catch." The 6'3", 197-pound receiver sometimes plays his position like a basketball rebounder, sweeping the ball off the "boards" for a touchdown. The basketball comparison has some merit. Cris' brother, Butch, toiled in the National Basketball Association for seven seasons.

In typical Carter style, he gives most of the credit for his spectacular '94 performance to Moon. "He's so good, so professional," says Carter. "He puts the ball where you need it. He makes my job so much easier to do."

Many pro football insiders credit last year's passing and receiving statistics to the tightened rules on downfield coverage. But a check of NFL statistics show that Carter wound up with 10 more receptions than any other receiver—and that includes San Francisco's Jerry Rice. The leading wide receiver in the AFC, Buffalo's Andre Reed, finished 32 catches behind Carter!

"I'm pleased with the new record," said Carter. "It was one of my goals before the season started. But how often do you reach a goal like that?"

For Carter, who has played in the last two Pro Bowls—the first two of his career—the goals will continue to grow.

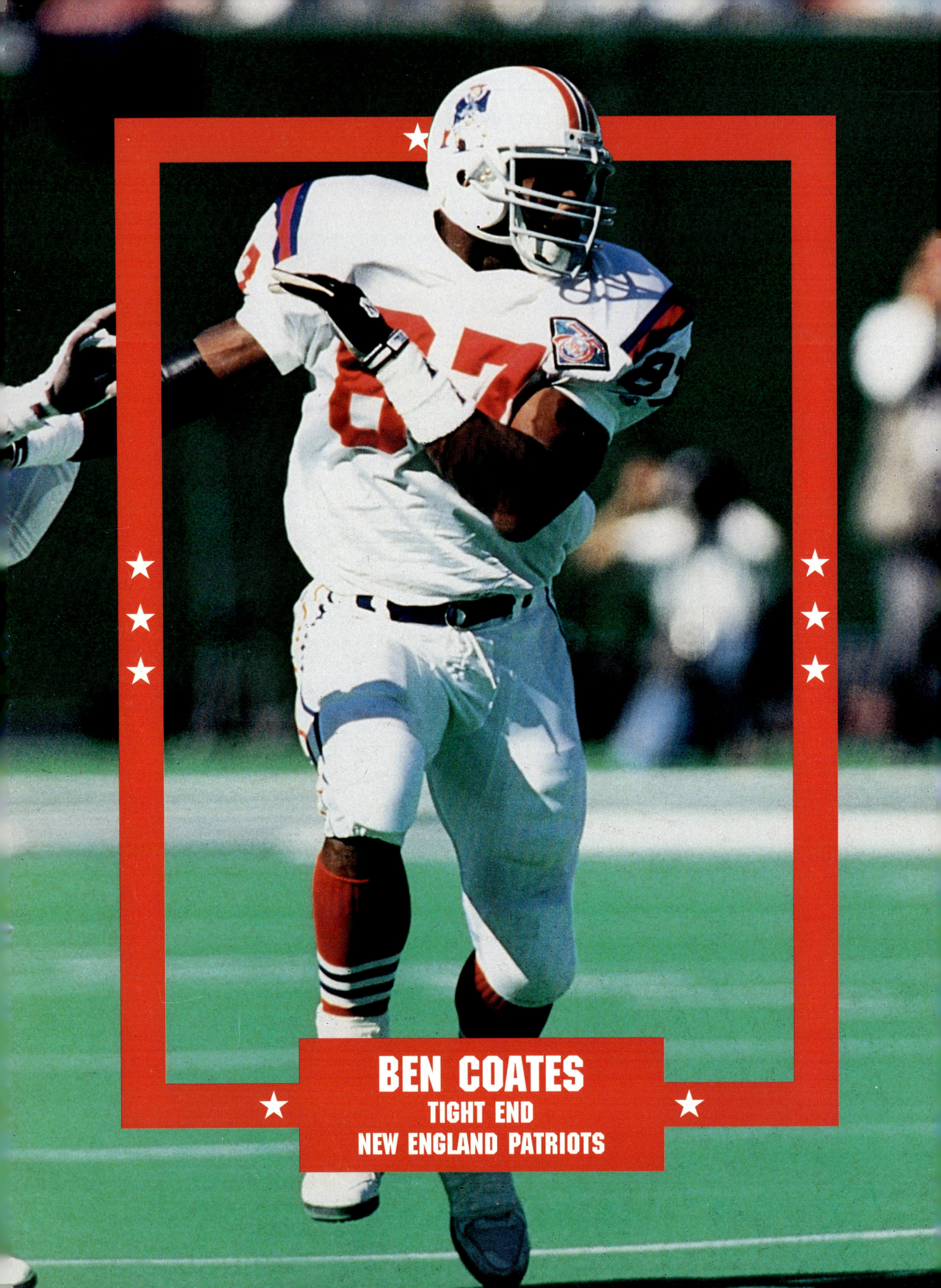

BEN COATES
TIGHT END
NEW ENGLAND PATRIOTS

No one ever said that Bill Parcells wasn't smart. Blessed with a two-time Pro Bowl tight end in Marv Cook, the New England Patriots field boss took one look at Cook's $850,000 salary and said good-bye. "Why not?" says Parcells. "I had Ben Coates." That 1993 post-season move may have helped the Pats to the top of the AFC East in '94.

It was Coates who forced Parcells into the move. Big Ben (he's 6'5" and weighs 245 pounds) goes deep, shrugs off tacklers after he catches the ball, and loves to pick up blitzing safeties trying to get at quarterback Drew Bledsoe. To Parcells, the choice was a no-brainer.

"When we were playing a conservative, move-the-chains offense," says Pats' tight end coach Charlie Weis, "Cook was just fine. But when we decided to abandon the tanks and fly with the bomber, we needed Ben. He's big and strong, blocks like a lineman, and can get deep."

Parcells likes everything about Coates, who came to the Pats from little-known Livingstone College in Salisbury, North Carolina. Ben grew up in Greenwood, South Carolina, originally a mill town until major manufacturers discovered the benefits of locating in the Palmetto State. Now, Greenwood turns out products for General Electric, Monsanto, and Fuji—and tight ends for the New England Patriots.

If you haven't heard of Greenwood, you're obviously not a college recruiter. The Greenwood High Eagles have long been a South Carolina power. When legendary coach Pinky Babb retired in 1981, he was the second-winningest coach in the nation. There are at least four Greenwood Eagles in the NFL today, a claim that few high schools can make. But when Ben was playing there, few dreamed that he'd be one of the most famous alumni. In fact, he's better remembered as a defensive back than as a tight end.

If the Greenwood coaches knew then what they know now, they might have redesigned their offense around their tight end. These days, Ben is the best tight end in the business and the best partner quarterback Drew Bledsoe has. "I'd like to throw to him on every play," says the QB. Against the Colts in Week 13 last year, he almost did. Ben caught a team-record 13 passes. And when Coates caught three passes for 26 yards in New England's 1994 finale against Chicago, he set a new single-season record for receptions by a tight end with 96. (The old record-holder: former Raider and current broadcaster, Todd Christiansen.)

Ben knows that he's fortunate to have wound up with the Pats. Around the NFL, Parcells is known as the guru of tight ends. Bill coached the classic tight end Mark Bavaro with the Giants and now has Bavaro's successor in Coates.

"I know the coach has helped make me a lot better," says Ben. "He has taught me to keep my head in the game at all times. I always have to be on the alert. Playing tight end in Parcells' offense is especially demanding, but he's really demanding of all the players."

Ben is equally fortunate that he arrived in Foxboro, Massachusetts, at the same time as QB Bledsoe. Drew is especially fond of throwing to Coates, and the pair threatens to become one of those famous pitch/catch teams, à la Joe Montana and Jerry Rice and, closer to home, Phil Simms and Bavaro.

"We work well together," says Coates. "He knows that against a blitz, I'm usually open as an outlet and I love it when he gets me open long."

Before you hang the genius label on Parcells for keeping Coates and dumping Cook, remember that Coates actually took over in '93. Given a couple of starts and plenty of playing time in his rookie year, he wound up with eight scores to lead the team. No Patriot tight end had scored as many touchdowns since All-Pro Russ Francis a decade and a half ago. Coates just missed tying that mark in '94 when he finished with seven. But his 96 catches (tops in the AFC) for 1,174 yards produced a nifty 12.3 yards-per-reception average.

Although Parcells freely admits that the team's offensive style is perfectly suited for a tight end like Ben, quarterback Bledsoe is equally convinced that any passer in the league would like to have Coates on his side.

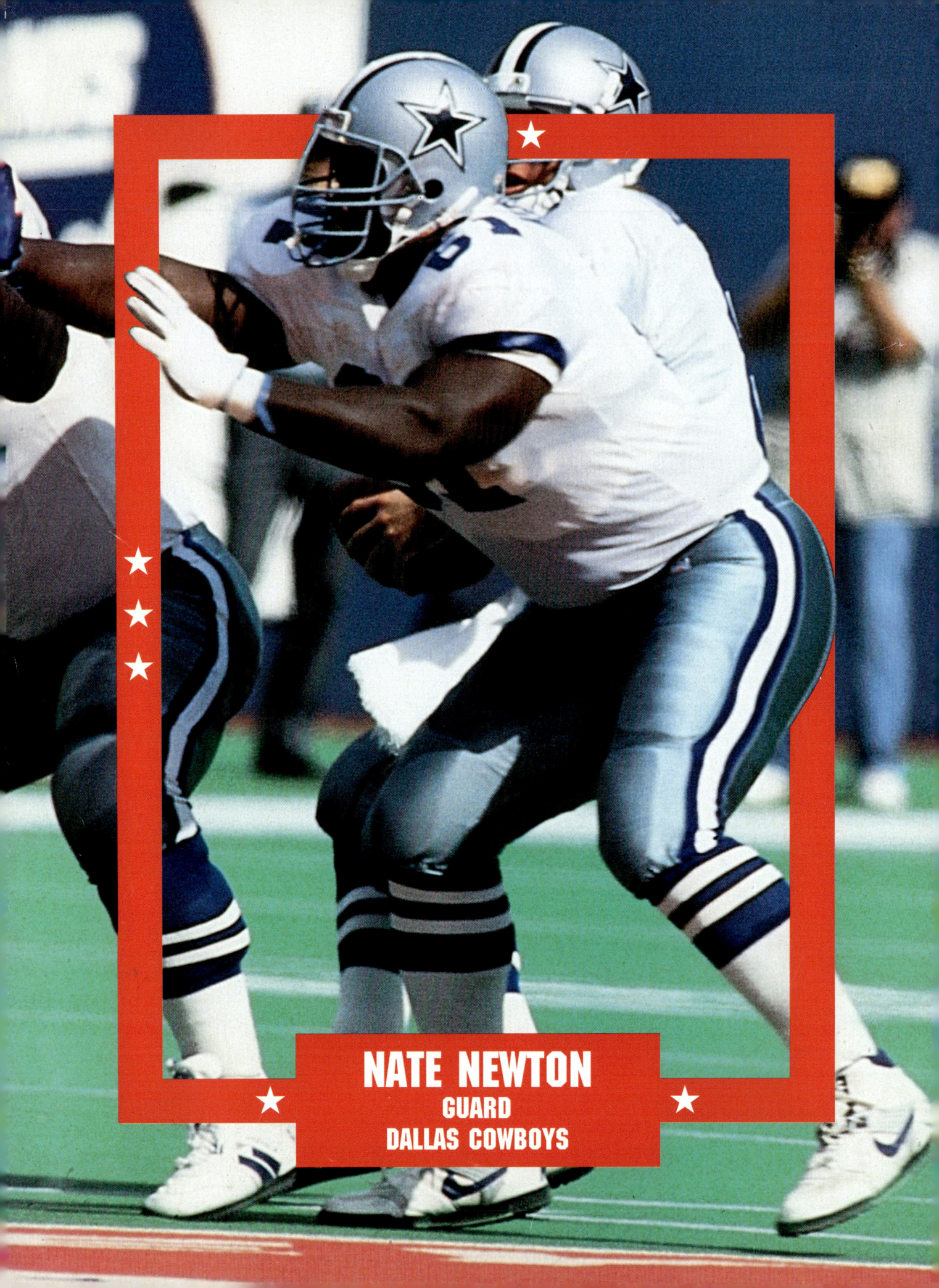

NATE NEWTON
GUARD
DALLAS COWBOYS

He isn't exactly slim. Roly-poly is still a working description. But Nate Newton, the Dallas Cowboys All-Pro (and All-Madden) guard, has become a teddy bear of a man, lovable, cuddly—and, just when you might have thought he'd lost it—still about the best guard in football.

Slim? Not at 6'3" and 335 pounds. But when you consider that the man has weighed up to 400 pounds during his football career, that's downright skinny. And he has become America's sweetheart on America's team. He's everyone's friend, everyone's role model. On the field, he's one of the toughest guys in the business, the blocker who saves Troy Aikman's life and opens holes for Emmitt Smith to pick. Off the field, he's the master of ceremonies. It's his locker that the press seeks for the light touch. And on a Cowboys flight home from a road victory, he's the team toastmaster, leading whatever hijinks the rest of the club can think up.

Of course, it wasn't always that way. In his younger days, Newton was something of a terror. A first-class, number-one bully. Just ask his high school and college classmates. They were terrified of him. Many of them, not believing there could be a new Nate Newton, still are. "He was the biggest guy around, he shaved his head before it became fashionable to do so, and looked and acted scary," says one. "He was frightening to see."

Hard to believe, but true. Nate grew up in Orlando, the son of a service station operator (Nate, Sr.) and a teacher (Margret). He never ran with gangs, never was a troublemaker. But once he hit the campus at Florida A&M, a predominantly black college with a great football tradition, things changed. He ragged on everyone, especially the female students, in a misguided effort to be funny. But his huge size frightened people and he didn't have many friends. Looking back, Nate realizes that this was his loss. He was taken as a fool, which he certainly isn't.

After a pretty decent career at A&M, Nate was ready for pro football. But football wasn't ready for Nate. No one selected him in the 1983 draft, but he signed as a free agent with the Washington Redskins. They cut him. Later the same evening, he was seriously injured in an auto accident.

Fortunately for Nate, he recovered. Equally fortunate, there was somewhere else for a prospective pro football player to go in the mid-1980s: the United States Football League. So Nate latched onto the Tampa Bay Bandits and played for two years, the entire life of the league. When the end came in 1986, he joined the Cowboys. He was not an overnight success. He endured long sessions of fat jokes and pictures. It was here that he earned his nickname, "The Kitchen." After all, the Cowboys reasoned, he was bigger than the Bears' William Perry, who was called "The Refrigerator."

Newton showed obvious football ability, but had considerable trouble with his weight, occasionally ballooning up to the 400-pound area and then dropping as low as 297. It took years for him to determine that his ideal playing weight is his current 335 pounds.

Despite his yo-yo dieting, Nate remained one of Dallas' strongest players, a statistic that fascinated the 'Boys' new coach, Jimmy Johnson, who arrived from the University of Miami in 1989. Johnson didn't care what a player looked like so long as he could play the game.

That suited Nate perfectly and he has blossomed into an every-year Pro Bowler since his move from tackle to guard three seasons ago. He's solid whether the team is employing area blocking or blocking one-on-one. And he pulls as well as any guard around.

He has also become one of the most expensive "Kitchens" in America. At age 33, he's now in the second year of a three-year, $3.4-million contract.

Newton's battle for weight control is never over. If you have the ability to be 400 pounds, maintaining 335 can be a struggle. But Nate's is one of the Cowboys' hardest off-season workouts (and the owner of his personal $2,000 exercise bike, a key ingredient in his weight-control plan).

Now his head seems fairly straight. "When I came here," he remembers, "I was the fat man and I was sort of unique. Now every team has a couple of guys who look like me. I guess I was just a pioneer."

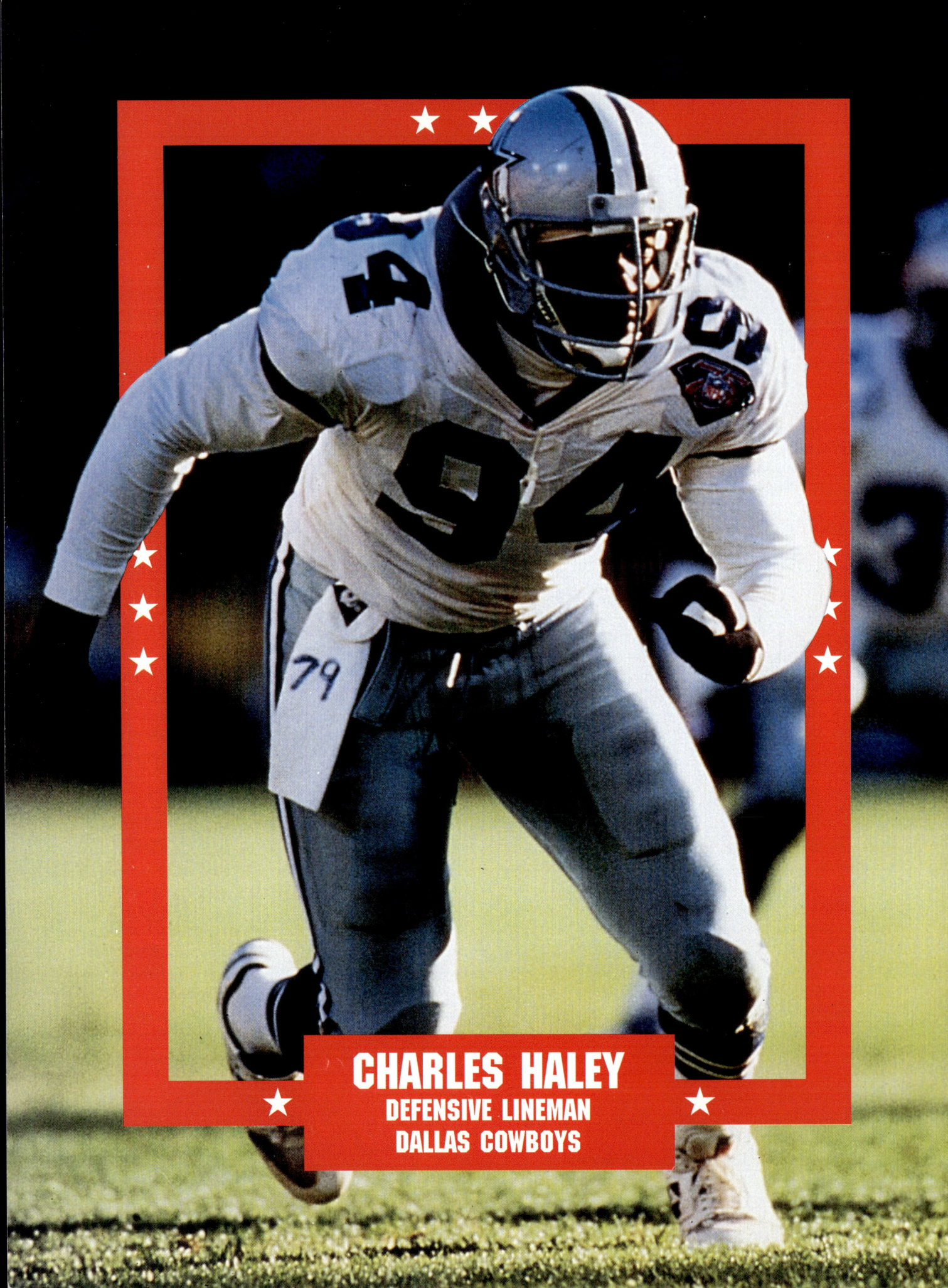

CHARLES HALEY
DEFENSIVE LINEMAN
DALLAS COWBOYS

★ THE COMET HALEY ★

f you think you've figured out Dallas Cowboys' defensive end Charles Haley, step to the front of the line. Through some mostly great years at San Francisco and Dallas, loads of people thought they had a handle on large Charles. But they're probably kidding themselves.

Talk to current and former teammates of the premier defensive end and you'll get an earful of varying opinions. The one theme that recurs, however, is that he's one of the smartest players in the game. For this, Haley credits playing with other smart players, including his one-time 49er teammates, Ronnie Lott and Keena Turner. Another 'Niner-turned-Fox-TV-analyst, Matt Millen, remembers a stream of criticism from Haley if he (Millen) ever made an error in calling a defense in the huddle.

Other 49er teammates remember the battling side of Haley. He fought with everyone, verbally and physically. He argued constantly with his defensive coordinator and later head coach, George Seifert. He came to blows with teammates Tim Harris and Jim Burt, among others. In the end, Seifert was moved to trade Haley to Dallas—for second- and third-round draft picks. It could have been the all-time basement bargain.

A bit undersized for an NFL defensive end (6'5" and 250 pounds, up from his rookie year 225), Haley makes up for it with superb quickness and his widely acknowledged smarts. There isn't a quarterback in the NFL who isn't concerned about having Haley in his face.

His incredible success as a pro came as a surprise to some who had watched him grow up as a football player. He was raised in Gladys, Virginia, by hardworking parents who labored day and night to feed Charles and his four brothers. Overlooked by major-college scouts, he went on to James Madison University, now a I-AA school probably best known as the current home of basketball coach Lefty Driesell.

The 'Niners took a shot picking him in the fourth round of the 1986 draft. The gamble paid almost instant dividends. By his third season, Charles was a Pro Bowler—and, to 49ers management, a royal pain. Still, they hung together long enough for Haley to win a couple of Super Bowl rings in the city by the bay.

The beginning of the end came in 1991, when the 'Niners allowed all-time defensive back Ronnie Lott to go to the Raiders as a free agent. Lott had been Haley's mentor in San Francisco. "When he left, in effect Charles left, too," recalls 49er president Carmen Policy.

Meanwhile in Dallas, owner Jerry Jones and coach Jimmy Johnson were building a championship club of their own. Problem was, their pass defense was awful, and pass defense begins with the front four. When Haley became available, they jumped at the chance. In Haley's first season with the Cowboys, the pass defense went from number 23 in the league to number 5. That's instant impact. That also helped Haley win his third Super Bowl ring—and a new three-year, big-bucks contract.

But Charles wasn't finished challenging the bosses. When the Cowboys lost their first two games in 1993 when Emmitt Smith was holding out for a bigger contract, Haley blew up. "What is this club thinking about?" he screamed for all to hear. "We need to get serious and get Emmitt in here!" He may have been uncomfortable about it, but owner Jones responded, signed Smith, and went on to win a second-straight Super Bowl.

The one thing you hear about Haley from everyone is that he has an incredible drive for perfection. That's why he's so hard on himself—and his teammates.

But he does have one enormous saving grace. Although he expects all of his line mates to work as hard as he does and play in as much pain as he does, he's always willing to work with them to overcome their errors. If he spots something in a game tape that needs fixing, he's out on the field later fixing it. Although the Cowboys defensive front of Tolbert, Maryland, Lett, and the rest is superbly talented, most will admit that Haley made them better players. And, above all, he's honest, brutally honest at times.

Unlike Forrest Gump's famous box of chocolates, with Charles Haley you always know—like it or not—exactly what you're going to get!

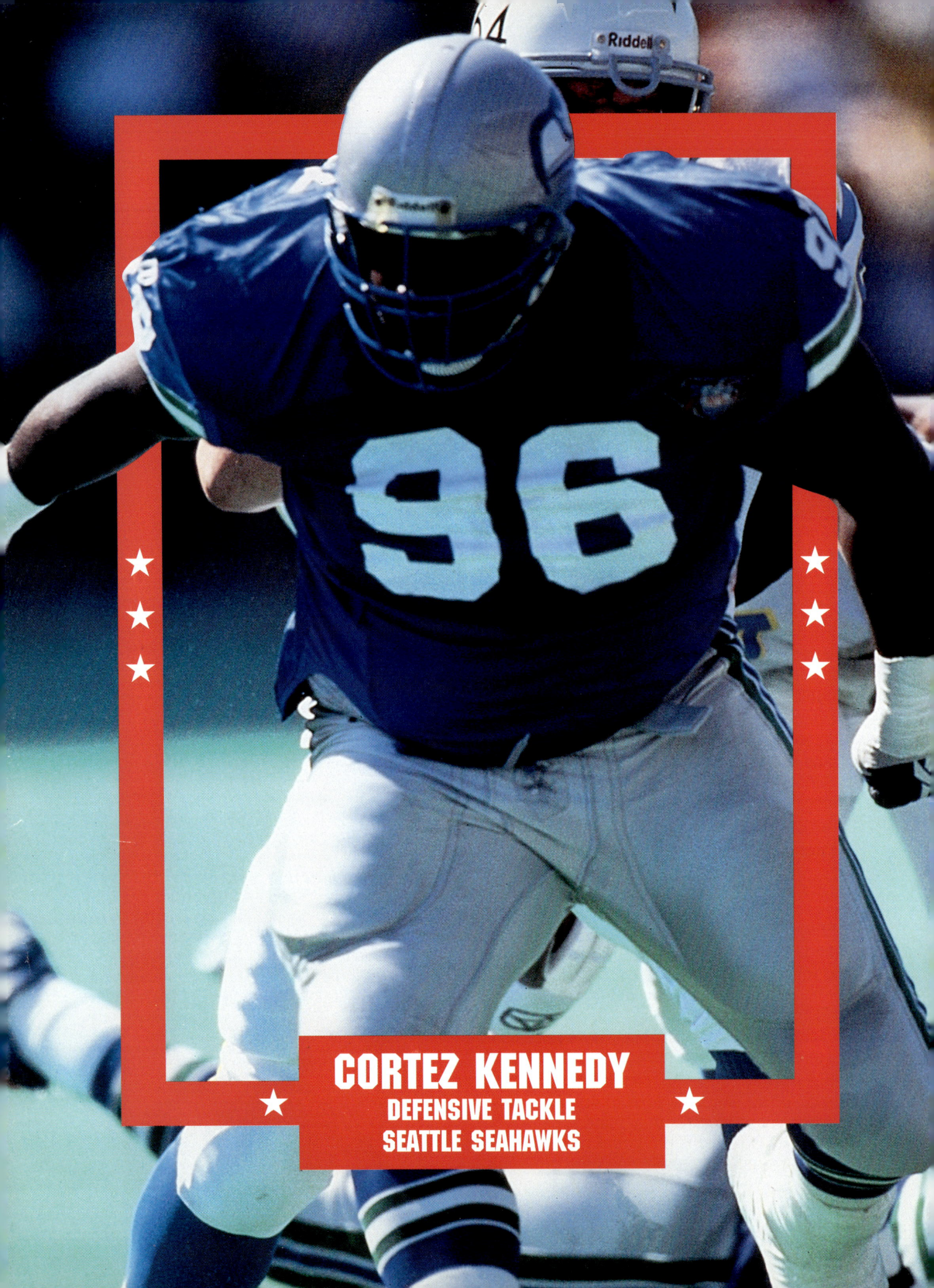

CORTEZ KENNEDY
DEFENSIVE TACKLE
SEATTLE SEAHAWKS

"My goals," says Cortez Kennedy, "are simple. I want to win a Super Bowl and I want to go to the Hall of Fame." There are folks in Seattle who think that Goal No. 1 is totally unrealistic. Goal No. 2, on the other hand, looks like a sure thing.

Five years ago, when Seattle selected the U. of Miami's Kennedy with the third pick in the NFL draft, they thought they were getting a player around whom they could build a rock-solid defense. They got everything they dreamed of—and more.

Fortunately for the man they call Tez, the draft was five and not six years ago. Until his senior year at Miami, Kennedy hadn't been doing much. He wasn't what you'd call a natural athlete. His body was closer to the Pillsbury Dough Boy than it was to a Greek god. For Kennedy, the NFL might as well have been playing on Mars.

That's when a couple of former Miami stars got into his head. The Dallas Cowboys Russell Maryland and the Philadelphia Eagles Jerome Brown convinced Tez that he had a future if he worked at it. That was all the motivation he needed.

He enjoyed a spectacular senior season, earning the early draft pick. Before he knew it, he was in the Pro Bowl, not believing he was there. "I remember telling Howie Long what a thrill it was to play with him there. He told me, 'Tez, it's an honor to play with you.' Wow!"

The only thing that can stop Cortez now is allowing himself to get out of shape. The Seahawks have made their bid to assure that it won't happen. His current $13-million contract actually contains a $200,000 bonus if he spends the off-season working out in Seattle.

Naturally, he'll never be a little guy, and that's good. His combination of size, speed, and quickness is virtually unmatched. "He's so big," raved former Denver head coach, Wade Phillips. And Kansas City offensive guard Dave Szott says, "What I can't believe is his strength. If he wants to go inside me, there's really little I can do to stop him."

The Seattle 4–3 set is perfectly suited to his talents. Instead of trying to stuff everything, as a 3–4 nose tackle needs to do, he can come off the ball, stopping the run and leading the force up the middle.

Even last season, probably not Tez's best as a pro, he was still the most dominating player at his position. He reminds most NFL insiders of the Dallas tackles who ruled the game for so long—Randy White and Bob Lilly. Both of them are enshrined at the Hall of Fame in Canton, Ohio. That's why we believe that Kennedy's second dream is so realistic. Some folks are alarmed that his 1994 sack total was only four, down from his 1992 club-record year of 14 (plus 28 tackles for negative yardage). But quickness doesn't go into a slump and that's the key to Tez's game.

If you looked at Kennedy without knowing his reputation, you'd wonder how good a football player he could be. Standing 6'1¾" and weighing around 300 pounds, he owns a legitimate gut. His football pants are size 46 and his jersey is XXL, and those garments barely hold him. But he squats around 600 pounds and has been timed as fast as 4.8 in the 40.

That he has made a success in the NFL comes as something of a surprise even to Kennedy. His academic performance in high school was so poor that his schoolteacher mom and construction company owner dad made him drop out of jayvee football at Rivercrest High School until he got his grades up. Even when he got his grades up, they weren't good enough to get him into a four-year college. So he played for Northwest Mississippi Junior College until he got that part of his game in order. Even at Miami U., his next stop, it took the urging of Brown and Maryland to really kick up to the next level. As a senior, Tez led all Miami linemen with 92 tackles and 7½ sacks. There was no stopping him after that.

With his on-field performance no longer in doubt, Kennedy is now poised to focus on the other part of his dream, that Super Bowl ring. With a new administration in place in Seattle, maybe—just maybe—it can happen.

MO LEWIS
LINEBACKER
NEW YORK JETS

★ OLD MO-MENTUM ★

Before you write letters to the publisher, read a little more. You're going to tell us that Mo Lewis didn't even make the Pro Bowl last February—and you're right. You're going to tell us that the Jets are awful—and you're right. But the second reason probably explains the first. Even more important, consider that most Pro Bowl linebackers are selected based on one statistic: sacks.

Unfortunately for Mo, the Jets' basic defensive scheme (hey, we didn't know they had one!) is a 4–3 (four linemen, three linebackers). In that set, Mo is the weakside 'backer, lining up in a stack (behind a defensive lineman) opposite an offensive guard and tackle. That keeps him from making those off-the-corner rushes at the quarterback, which turn other linebackers into sack masters. The Jets would love to get Mo into the pass rush. But they need him more to stuff the run and cover tight ends and backs on pass plays.

When Pro Bowl voters selected the AFC team, they opted for the sack guys. Pittsburgh's Greg Lloyd had 14 at the time, his teammate Kevin Greene had 10, as did the Chiefs' Derek Thomas. Mo had only 2½ at that time.

Oddly, Lewis came to the Jets with a reputation as a fearsome pass-rusher. He was a high school terror at Atlanta's J.C. Murphy and, at the University of Georgia, he once had 10 sacks in an 11-game season. That made him a valuable commodity and the Jets made him their third-round pick in the 1991 draft.

But New York had a bigger role in mind for the 6'3", 255-pound Lewis. They wanted him to enhance all of his skills—and he has done it. Given his size and his nose for the football, he's outstanding against the run. But in terms of the speed and agility needed to cover passes downfield, Lewis sacrifices nothing.

Last year he wound up as the Jets' team leader in tackles with 138, more than 100 of them solos. He also forced 3 fumbles, made 11 tackles for losses, and had 4 interceptions. Making like an oversized Deion Sanders, he returned two of the interceptions for Jets' touchdowns. And this guy didn't make the Pro Bowl.

As for sacks, in the 1994 season finale at Houston, he more than doubled his total for the first 15 games of the year. His three QB dumps

that day gave him 5½ for the season. Maybe the Pro Bowl voters should have asked for a recount.

Mo's performance won him more than a few admirers. The Packers general manager, Ron Wolf, is among them. "Whatever you're looking for in a linebacker," says Wolf, "Mo has. He can rush the QB, play the pass, or stuff the ball at the line." Patriots' coach Bill Parcells agrees. He ought to know. New England's Big Tuna coached the supreme outside 'backer, Lawrence Taylor, when Taylor was with the Giants. "Mo was one of the best linebackers in the league last season," said Parcells. "He got my Pro Bowl vote."

At age 26, Lewis is at the top of his game. Last season was his best as a pro, and he only figures to get better. The rave reviews come from teammates and opponents alike. Donald Evans, who came to the Jets from Pittsburgh a year ago, likens Lewis to a "bigger and younger Greg Lloyd." And Evans played with Lloyd, the AFC's leading sacker last year, for many seasons. Another 1994 teammate, future Hall of Fame safety Ronnie Lott, is impressed with Lewis' multiple talents. "He reminds me of a couple of guys I played with in San Francisco—Charles Haley and Fred Dean. We ask those players to do so many things, drop to cover the pass, rush the QB, and stuff the run. Look at how many tackles Mo made for losses last year. That takes quickness and strength, and that's Mo's game."

Although Lewis was visibly upset over his Pro Bowl snub, he wasn't about to ask the Jets to change anything. A black belt in karate, Mo would love nothing more than to chase quarterbacks all over the Meadowlands. But he's realistic. "If I tried to specialize, like in rushing the passer, I'd lose my versatility. That would mean I wouldn't live up to my potential. And that I won't do."

While the Jets have lots of work to do to rebuild a team that crumbled late (again!) in '94, new coach Rich Kotite knows he's set at weakside linebacker.

DEION SANDERS
DEFENSIVE BACK
SAN FRANCISCO 49ERS

Last summer's major-league baseball strike might have been the best thing that ever happened to the San Francisco 49ers. When the Atlanta Falcons, tired of sharing Deion Sanders with baseball, waived the All-Pro cornerback, Neon Deion became the instant star of football's version of *America's Most Wanted*. As so often happens, the 'Niners came out on top.

Only a few months earlier, Deion announced that he was done with football. "I feel like I'm twenty-six going on thirty-six," said the two-sport superstar. Football, he felt, would make him an old man before his time.

Then two things happened, both of them good for the NFL. First, remember that Deion makes lots of announcements. Few of them amount to much. Second, the baseball strike, which led to the cancellation of the end of the season, gave Sanders too much time on his hands. If not for the strike, there's no telling what Deion would have done. Traded from the Atlanta Braves to the Cincinnati Reds last May, he was enjoying his best season ever when the players walked out. He was hitting .283 and had racked up 38 stolen bases when the semi-season concluded.

Most sports experts concede that Michael Jordan is the finest athlete in the nation. But the greatest basketball player ever could barely hit .200 as a minor-league baseball player. Sanders, now a solid big-league outfielder, is one of the most feared defensive backs ever in the NFL.

What got Deion excited about playing football again? The chance to win a championship. "When we got down to the final games of the season in Atlanta, we were always out of it," says Sanders. "I really didn't have my heart in it at the end. That's why I picked San Francisco. I knew they'd be in it all the way and there were other superstars to share the pressure. I didn't have to be the main man all the time."

Like so many great players, Sanders makes those around him play better, too. For example, San Francisco safety Merton Hanks had seven interceptions last season. Having Deion in the backfield with him had to help. Sanders had six INTs himself and, more important, he returned half of them—three—for touchdowns.

Deion has every ingredient a cornerback needs: toughness, quickness, incredible speed, consistency, enormous self-confidence, and great football instincts. He has flash and style (which you either love or hate).

He also owns the biggest mouth in pro sports. He never met a thought that he wasn't willing to blurt out on a moment's notice or a person he wasn't anxious to pass judgment on.

Add Atlanta Falcons' wide receiver Andre Rison to Sanders' list. When the 'Niners and Falcons met last fall, the game sunk to a new low when the former teammates engaged in some serious slap-fighting—which the officials basically ignored. That didn't stop Deion from shooting from the lip. Nothing does. He followed the fight with a 93-yard interception return for six points. And when San Francisco matched up with defending Super Bowl champion Dallas a couple of weeks later, Deion led a secondary that defensed seven Troy Aikman passes. The Cowboys, on the other hand, defensed only one Steve Young toss. That's the kind of player Sanders is: The bigger the reputation of his opponent, the better he plays.

Where does Deion go from here? Who knows? Even if he tells you, chances are you can't believe him. When he signed with San Francisco, it was strictly a one-year deal. Deion himself says, "I'm a baseball player." That's too bad, because if he were a football player, they could probably dust off a spot for his statue at the Hall of Fame in Canton, Ohio.

Of course, Sanders' future might not be in football or baseball. Although he says "sports is what I live for," he occasionally thinks his future is in music. He cut a rap album and, of course, it was named for him, *Prime Time*. And he took off after some of his previous targets, baseball announcer Tim McCarver and movie director Spike Lee. But his self-confidence poured out in his signature rap, "You Can't Stop the Prime Time."

Most folks would love to have Deion's choices. He can't do badly whichever way he goes. But for Deion Sanders, even the simplest statement is bound to be controversial.

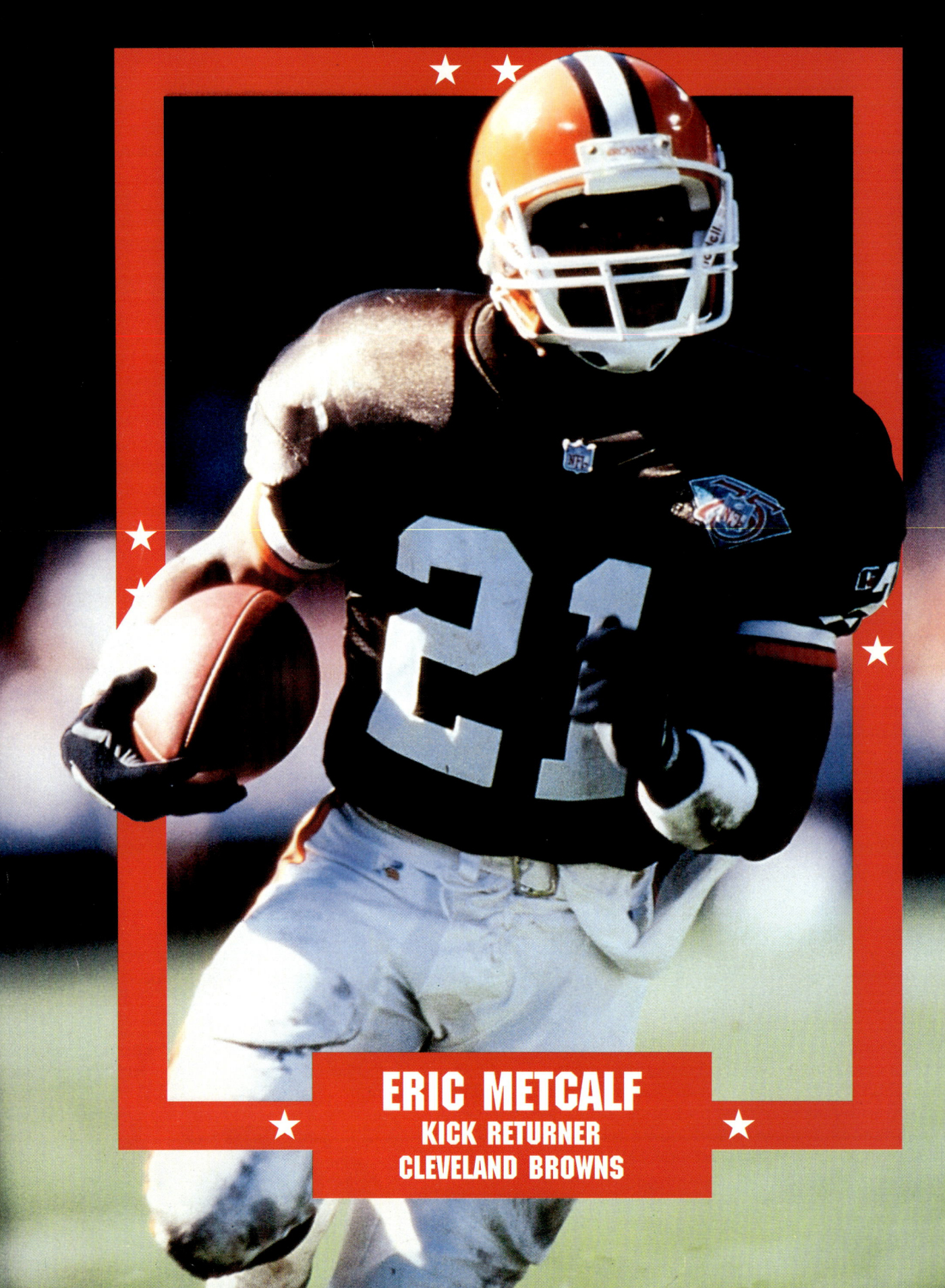

ERIC METCALF
KICK RETURNER
CLEVELAND BROWNS

★ FATHERS AND SONS ★

Serious students of heredity, please note: Make the National Football League your next research project. To succeed as a kick returner, it's becoming increasingly obvious that it helps to have had a father who was a great runner.

Our megastar, Cleveland's Eric Metcalf, is the son of one of the Cardinals' all-time great RBs, Terry Metcalf. In the NFC, the main man is Mel Gray of the Detroit Lions, son of another immortal, also named Mel Gray.

Metcalf is the most frightening player in the Cleveland lineup. Power back Leroy Hoard returns this year off a superb 1994 (890 yards on 209 carries). Quarterback Vinny Testaverde hasn't scared anyone since his final year at the University of Miami. And the high-octane Cleveland defense, molded carefully by coach Bill Belichick, is a team effort.

So it's Metcalf—and only Metcalf—who can beat you on any play. He has been doing it since he arrived at Cleveland Stadium in 1989 as the Browns' first draft choice. His reputation preceded him. At the University of Texas, he was voted the offensive player of the '80s. That's right, the whole decade. He set a Southwest Conference record for all-purpose (rushing, receiving, punt return, kickoff return) yardage with 5,703. Since the Southwest Conference is in the process of going out of business, here's a record that absolutely will live forever. It didn't count in his record total, but he also threw for a pair of touchdowns. If there was any doubt about Eric's athletic ability, he ended that by winning a pair of NCAA long-jump titles, including a world-class leap of 27'2" as a junior.

Now, six seasons later, he remains the king of all-purpose yardage. Though his numbers were down a bit last year, possibly because of the emergence of Hoard as the Browns' battering ram, Eric still frightens opponents every time he touches the ball.

If you need proof, just ask the Cincinnati Bengals. He owns them. In last year's first meeting on opening day, with the Browns' offense struggling, Metcalf personally turned things around. In what may be the world's ultimate contact sport, he did it without any contact whatsoever.

Metcalf waited for Lee Johnson's punt on his own eight yard line. He knew that a right return had been called in the huddle. That meant that the blockers would set up their picket fence on the right sideline.

As Metcalf made the catch, he looked up and saw that the fence had been set up just as it was drawn on the locker room blackboard. If he could be the first man, if he could get to the corner, he might be able to pick up major yardage.

Eric knew what he was doing. It wasn't anything he hadn't seen before. In fact, against Pittsburgh in '93, he returned punts for 91 and 75 yards in the same game. In the 75-year history of the NFL, no one had ever returned two punts for 75 yards or more in the same game.

It surprised no one in Cincinnati last September that Metcalf managed to get past the first wave of Bengals. But when he got to the corner and looked up, a smile creased his face. All over the field, the guys in the white shirts were putting the guys in the black shirts on the ground. Metcalf zipped down the field. No Bengal laid a finger on him. When teammate Eric Thomas blocked punter Johnson, Cincinnati's last defender, Metcalf was home free.

That was the first of two Metcalf TD returns in '94, giving him four in two years and, including kickoff returns, seven return scores in his career. That puts him in the NFL's all-time top eight in kick returns. In addition, he's one of only two Browns ever to score on a punt, a kickoff, a rush, a pass, and by throwing a TD pass. The other is Hall of Famer Bobby Mitchell.

Eric's dad, Terry, the old Cardinal star, is extraordinarily proud of his son's achievements. "When I see films of Eric, it's like looking in the mirror," says Terry. "It's like reliving my life."

As good as Terry was, the feeling here is that Eric is even better. When he struts into the end zone after another lengthy scamper with a kick, he's really in a class by himself.

JOHN CARNEY
PLACEKICKER
SAN DIEGO CHARGERS

★ CARNEY-VAL IN SAN DIEGO ★

There aren't many pro football megastars who have to fill their pockets to get the scale to tip up to 170 pounds. So we must be talking about a kicker. Of course, you're right. But this isn't about any kicker; it's about John Carney, who makes people in San Diego smile, on and off the field.

The folks in southern California (and, we suppose, northern Mexico) love him. A one-time Cub Scout who rides Harley-Davidson motorcycles and wears Harley-Davidson clothes, John has become a vital member of the Chargers community. Most placekickers never do.

That's the problem with the job. You're only as good as your last kick. With some of the flightier head coaches in the NFL, a bad week for a kicker can get him fired. That's the nature of things. In the age of the kicking specialist, you're only as good as last week's 48-yarder.

It wasn't always that way. Ask your grandpa. A generation or two ago, the placekicker needed to do something else to keep his roster spot. The Giants' Pat Summerall, now the lead broadcaster for Fox Television, was the kicker—and the wide receiver. The Browns' Lou Groza, whose nickname was "The Toe," was also an All-Pro tackle.

Forget that. These days, a kicker kicks—and that's it. The one thing he doesn't have is job security. Carney, who owns most of the Chargers' all-time kicking records, knows full well about that.

John remembers 1990: Graduated from Notre Dame. Signed by the Cincinnati Bengals. Cut by the Cincinnati Bengals. Signed by the Tampa Bay Buccaneers. Cut by the Tampa Bay Buccaneers. Signed by the Chargers and—that's right—cut by the Chargers.

When John arrived in San Diego, he found himself in a kicking duel with Fuad Reveiz. He lost it. No one picked him up. His pro career was over before it started. And then it wasn't. In the Chargers' first four games, Reveiz made two field goals—and missed five. Good-bye, Fuad; hello, John. Carney hit on 19 of his 21 field goal attempts, setting a Charger record with a .905 percentage. The rest is history.

In 1994, John led the AFC in scoring with 122 points. He hit on 29 of 29 extra points and 31 of 35 field goal attempts. Only one NFL kicker

outscored him. You guessed it. The scoring leader, with 125 points, was the Minnesota Vikings' Fuad Reveiz!

Even now, with success (but never job security) assured, John still looks back at his miraculous comeback of 1990. "I suppose I had faith in my ability and faith that God had a plan for me," he says. "I was never worried. If it wasn't the NFL, it would be something else. I had a degree from a respected college. So I would have been John Carney, businessman. But before I did that, I wanted to make certain that I couldn't make it in pro football. I just stuck with it."

The Chargers' reward for John's patience has been the most consistent kicker in the league. His career percentage (127 for 161, .789) ranks him among the top six of all time. Lack of an overwhelming offense in San Diego has given him more opportunities than most kickers. He has gone six-for-six twice, providing all of San Diego's points in their first two 1993 victories. He came back to hit five against New Orleans in '94, again personally securing a Charger victory. Carney set an NFL record by hitting 29 in a row during the 1992 and '93 seasons. Only a 48-yard wide-right miss against the Seattle Seahawks spoiled the streak.

What does it take to be a great NFL kicker? "It's mostly in the mental approach," says Charger field boss Bobby Ross. "There are lots of kickers with strong legs. It's the guys who keep their heads on straight who succeed."

One of the problems for the kickers is the constant spotlight shining on them. "An offensive lineman can blow five out of every thirty plays and no one knows it," says Ross. "But a kicker is out there all alone. If he blows one, everyone knows it. It's like playing defensive back. If you make a mistake, it's six points against you. It's tough.

"These days, we simply expect John to do it every time he goes out there. You know there are so many problems that can ruin the attempt. But you develop a high comfort level with him. When you think about it, is there anyone out there who's better than he is?"

BRUCE WEBER PICKS
HOW THEY'LL FINISH IN '95

NFC EAST
1. Dallas Cowboys
2. New York Giants
3. Arizona Cardinals
4. Washington Redskins
5. Philadelphia Eagles

NFC CENTRAL
1. Chicago Bears
2. Green Bay Packers
3. Detroit Lions
4. Minnesota Vikings
5. Tampa Bay Buccaneers

NFC WEST
1. San Francisco 49ers
2. New Orleans Saints
3. Atlanta Falcons
4. The Rams
5. Carolina Panthers

AFC EAST
1. New England Patriots
2. Miami Dolphins
3. Indianapolis Colts
4. Buffalo Bills
5. New York Jets

AFC CENTRAL
1. Pittsburgh Steelers
2. Cleveland Browns
3. Houston Oilers
4. Jacksonville Jaguars
5. Cincinnati Bengals

AFC WEST
1. Los Angeles Raiders
2. San Diego Chargers
3. Kansas City Chiefs
4. Seattle Seahawks
5. Denver Broncos

NFC CHAMPIONS: Dallas Cowboys

AFC CHAMPIONS: New England Patriots

SUPERBOWL XXX: Dallas 31, New England 17

YOU PICK HOW THEY'LL FINISH IN '95

NFC EAST
1._____
2._____
3._____
4._____
5._____

NFC CENTRAL
1._____
2._____
3._____
4._____
5._____

NFC WEST
1._____
2._____
3._____
4._____
5._____

AFC EAST
1._____
2._____
3._____
4._____
5._____

AFC CENTRAL
1._____
2._____
3._____
4._____
5._____

AFC WEST
1._____
2._____
3._____
4._____
5._____

NFC CHAMPIONS: _____

AFC CHAMPIONS: _____

SUPERBOWL XXX: _____

32